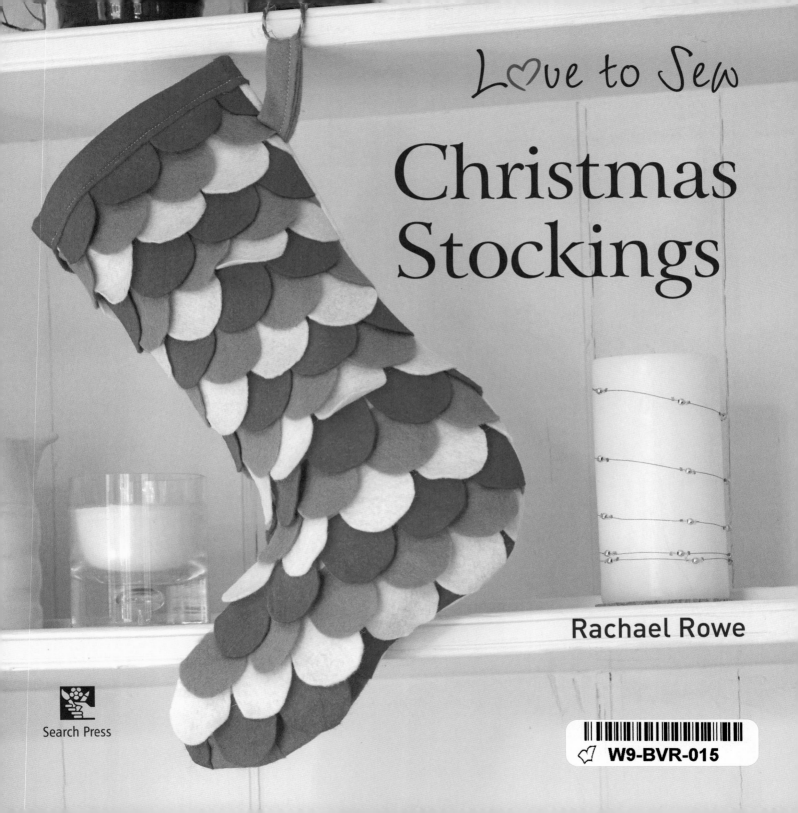

Love to Sew

Christmas Stockings

Rachael Rowe

Search Press

First published in Great Britain 2015

Search Press Limited
Wellwood, North Farm Road,
Tunbridge Wells, Kent TN2 3DR

Text copyright © Rachael Rowe 2015

Photographs by Paul Bricknell on location and at Search Press studios

Photographs and design copyright © Search Press Ltd. 2015

ISBN: 978-1-84448-974-9

The Publishers and author can accept no responsibility for any consequences arising from the information, advice or instructions given in this publication.

Suppliers
If you have difficulty in obtaining any of the materials and equipment mentioned in this book, then please visit the Search Press website for details of suppliers:
www.searchpress.com

You are invited to visit the author's website:
www.graceandfavourhome.com

Acknowledgements

The publishers would like to thank Rebecca Clibbens for kindly allowing us to use her house as a location for photography.

Patterns

All the stocking patterns are provided in a pocket inside the back cover.

Printed in China

Bauble Felt, page 20

Snowflake Appliqué, page 22

Pompom Cuff, page 24

Mini Initial, page 26

Scalloped Felt, page 28

Stitched Tree, page 30

Advent Calendar, page 32

Snowman, page 34

Toy Sack, page 36

Upcycled Sweater, page 38

Hand-Stitched Felt, page 40

Quilted Patchwork, page 42

Ric-Rac Panels, page 44

Hessian Initial, page 46

Appliqué Trees, page 48

Gorgeous Gifts, page 50

Pompoms Galore, page 52

Contents

Big Bow, page 54

Introduction

Christmas can be a wonderful, magical time for adults and children alike, and the traditions that lead up to the main event create memories to last a lifetime – choosing a tree, displaying the decorations and hanging up stockings on Christmas Eve, ready to be filled with treasures and trinkets. In this book, I show you a variety of projects to create your own special stockings for family, friends and loved ones, that will be cherished and brought out year after year.

There is a mixture of machine and hand-sewing projects in the book – some are more suited to those short on time (is it December already?!) while others require a little more planning and time to create something very personal, but all are fun and straightforward to make.

From simple hand-stitched felt, to appliqué, pompoms and bows, each project is a different take on the traditional Christmas stocking. I have made suggestions for colour and fabric through my own versions – but the huge variety of festive-themed fabrics available will enable you to put your own stamp on the heirlooms of the future. Pick colours, designs and trimmings to suit your own Christmas colour scheme, or that of the recipient.

Materials & equipment

As craft and sewing continue to enjoy stratospheric growth in popularity, so does the range of Christmas-themed fabrics and trimmings available to shoppers online and in store. From the more traditional Christmas themes, to simple 'Scandinavian' inspired motifs, and modern, geometric designs – there is so much choice, whether you wish for muted reds and greens, or bright pops of colour.

Fabrics

The majority of fabrics used in the projects in this book are cottons or cotton mixes designed for craft and dressmaking – they are lightweight but strong. If you are mixing fabrics within a project, it is always best to choose fabrics of a similar weight and feel, to ensure the end result looks as good as possible. Felt is used throughout this book and is a great material for less confident sewers – it doesn't fray and is hardwearing and forgiving. Do remember to look at the felt composition – many felts are manmade, so can withstand only very low iron temperature – it is always best to check and avoid a ruined iron.

Some of the projects use wadding/batting to create a quilted effect – this is readily available from your local sewing shop and comes in a variety of weights – use the lightest weight for the stockings – it will give the required effect without making the stocking too bulky.

Threads

The threads used throughout the book are standard polyester machine sewing threads, available on reels and cones from all sewing and craft shops. When sewing a project where the majority of sewing is functional, and on the inside, it is always best to match the colour of the thread to the fabric as closely as possible. For top stitching detail, you might like to try a contrasting colour for extra interest, though bear in mind this will be far more visible if your lines are a little wonky!

For the hand-sewn or embroidered projects, I have used standard embroidery threads/floss, which are available in a huge range of wonderful colours and finishes.

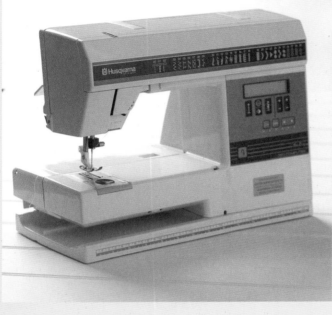

Sewing machine

For all the machine-stitched projects, you need a basic sewing machine that is capable of a straight stitch, with a backstitch function for finishing off the beginning and end of each stitch line. Use a medium-length stitch and adjust the tension according to the fabric being used.

Embellishments

The embellishments used in this book are a very small selection of the wonderful items available. I have used a mixture of satin ribbons, ric-rac, pompom trim and scraps of felt to create the projects – the choice for yours, though, is really up to you. With buttons, I have opted for mother-of-pearl and rustic wooden buttons to tie in with the project themes, but you might opt for bright colours and striking shapes. Your local fabric or craft shop should have a great selection – pick the ones that really catch your eye and you can't go wrong.

Other materials

You will need sharp **fabric scissors** to cut out the shapes in the projects. Never use the same scissors to cut paper or anything else. You will also need some small, sharp **embroidery scissors** for trimming and clipping curves, and **pinking shears** will be helpful for some projects.

A **tape measure** or **ruler** and **chalk** or a **fabric-marking pen** will also be useful. Keep a **seam ripper** handy to undo any mistakes.

I recommend standard **hand-sewing needles** for the majority of the machine-stitched projects, where the only hand sewing required is to sew the opening of the stocking lining closed, or to sew on embellishments such as buttons. For hand-stitched and embroidered projects, you will require an **embroidery needle** with a large eye and a fairly sharp point.

When pinning your work, use **dressmakers' pins** with a ball/pearl head, so they are very visible. Pin the fabric at right angles to your intended stitch line so you can stitch over the pins without damaging the sewing-machine needle.

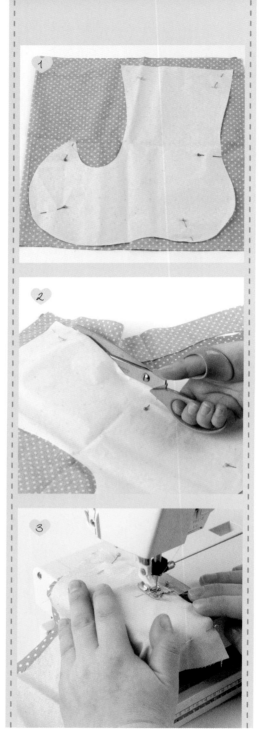

Making the basic stocking

The projects in this book all follow the same basic techniques and method. Most are lined to provide a neat finish on the inside, which is explained here. Any variations are detailed in the project instructions.

Materials

- ♥ stocking pattern B (without cuff)
- ♥ fabric for outer stocking, 52 x 66cm (20½ x 26in)
- ♥ fabric for hanging loop, 4 x 15cm (1½ x 6in)
- ♥ fabric for lining 52 x 66cm (20½ x 26in)

Tools

- ♥ pins
- ♥ fabric scissors
- ♥ thread

1 Take your outer stocking fabric and fold it in half, right sides together. All the patterns for the stockings are provided on a sheet in a pocket at the back of the book. Trace, photocopy or scan and print the stocking pattern then cut it out to make a template. In this example, use stocking pattern B without the cuff. Pin the template on with the pins at right angles to the edge of the pattern as shown.

2 Cut out with sharp fabric scissors against the edge of the template. Repeat these steps for your lining fabric.

3 Place the front of your stocking and the corresponding lining piece right sides together and pin along the top edge. Sew together with a 1cm (³⁄₈in) seam allowance. Repeat for the back of the stocking. Make sure the 'toes' of the outer and lining fabric point in the same direction. You will need to finish with two pieces that mirror each other (piece 1 with toes pointing to the left, piece 2 with toes pointing to the right).

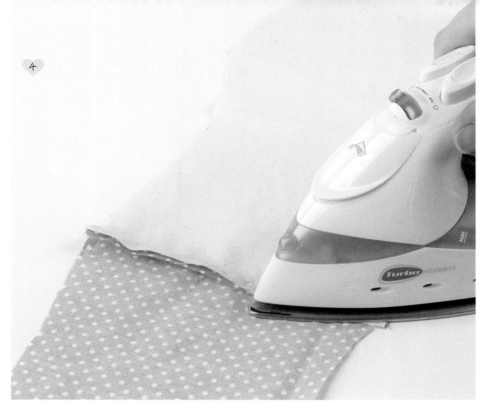

4 Press both seam allowances towards the toe of the stocking outer fabric and repeat with other piece.

5 To make the hanging loop (which will be attached when the stocking is stitched together), fold the fabric in half lengthwise and iron.

6 Open out and iron the edges in to the centre fold line as shown below.

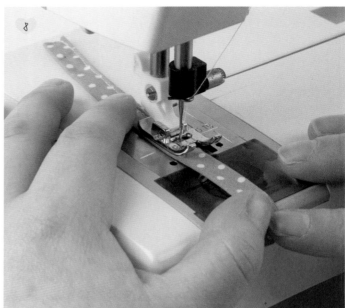

_7_ Fold the piece in half lengthwise again and iron.

_8_ Sew in place with a small machine stitch, close to the edge of the fabric.

_9_ Place the two stocking pieces with their main fabric and lining elements right sides together, matching the seams. Fold the hanging loop in half and place, as shown, just below the seam on the outer fabric with the looped end facing inwards and the raw edges in line with the edge of the stocking.

10 Pin the hanging loop in place and then pin through all layers round the outside of the stocking. Sew round, backstitching at the beginning and end of the seam line. Make sure you leave a gap in the lining big enough to fit your hand through.

11 Clip into the curves with sharp embroidery scissors, as this improves the shape when it is turned through. Snip with the scissors up to just short of the stitching line, taking out small triangular pieces, but don't cut through the thread.

12 Snip off the point of the stocking, at the main fabric and lining ends. Again, snip to just short of the stitching line.

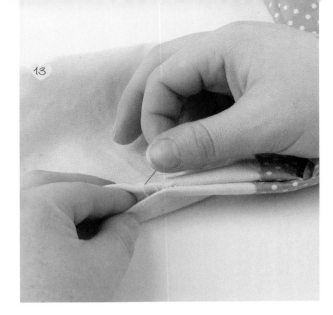

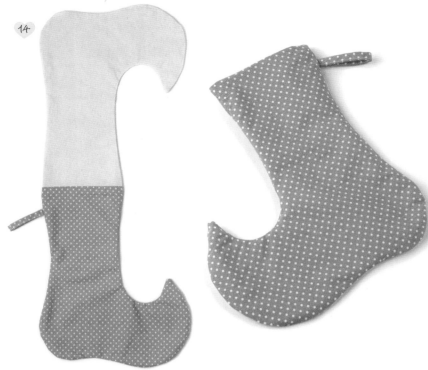

13 Turn through neatly, gently rolling the seams to enhance the shape. Hand stitch the opening closed.

14 Push the lining inside the stocking to finish, making sure to push right into the toe.

Making a felt hanging loop

As an alternative to the hanging loop instructions already shown, you can make one from felt. Cut a piece of felt 3 x 15cm (1¼ x 6in). Fold the piece in half lengthways, pin in place and sew down one side, close to the edge.

Using fusible web

Fusible web is great for creating neat, professional looking appliqué patches for your stockings – it helps the fabric to keep its shape and prevents it from getting stretched or puckered when you sew it in place.

1 Cut a piece of fusible web slightly bigger than your appliqué motif, and place it, paper side up, on the reverse of your appliqué fabric. Iron it in place, making sure it has stuck fully.

2 Draw your motif onto the paper, either with a template (here I have used template 14, on page 60) or freehand. Remember to create this in reverse as you will flip it over to apply it (particularly important for letters). Cut out your shape.

3 Peel off the backing paper and place the appliqué shape, web side down, on your background fabric. Make sure it is exactly where you want it, as once you iron it, you won't be able to remove it. Iron in place, pressing all over the shape. Secure with stitching, either by machine or hand.

Projects

On the following pages you will find eighteen projects to inspire you for the Christmas season – from traditional festive and winter scenes using appliqué and hand embellishment, to more contemporary designs which really let the wonderful fabrics shine. Each project is explained step by step, building on the techniques explained earlier. Every stocking is based on one of the patterns provided in a pocket at the back of the book. Some of the projects require additional templates and motifs which can be found on pages 57–64. The templates are all shown full size and simply need to be photocopied, traced or scanned into a computer and printed out.

At the start of each project, a complete list of materials and tools is provided, including quantities and sizes. I have chosen fabrics that complement the designs and techniques used, but you can use these as a starting point for your own style and creativity and opt for something completely different.

If you are making multiple stockings for your family or friends, why not create personalised variations of the same design, or pick completely opposite styles to reflect different personalities? Whatever you choose, I hope you will enjoy making the projects and creating memories for the future.

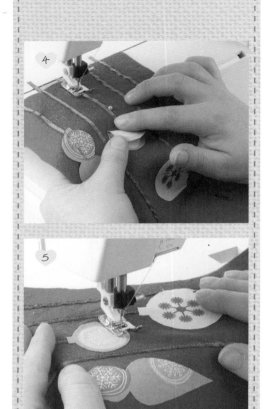

Bauble Felt

Materials

- stocking pattern B (without cuff)
- templates 1, 2, 3, 4 and 5 (page 57)
- felt for outer stocking, 39 x 66cm (15½ x 26in)
- felt for hanging loop, 3 x 15cm (1¼ x 6in)
- lengths of 3mm (⅛in) wide ribbon
- small pieces of patterned fabric for baubles
- fusible web
- thread

Tools

- scissors
- pins
- sewing machine

1 Take your stocking outer fabric and fold it in half, right sides together. Pin on stocking pattern B and cut out, leaving out the cuff part.

2 To create the baubles, iron fusible web on to the reverse of your small fabric pieces and draw round templates 1, 2, 3, 4 and 5 on page 57. Cut out.

3 Leaving the paper backing on the baubles, arrange on the felt stocking front piece and pin in place. Take lengths of ribbon and arrange in place to 'hang' the baubles from. Pin these in place.

4 Sew the ribbon in place, taking care not to sew over the baubles, but tucking the ribbon underneath each bauble edge.

5 Remove the pins and the backing from the baubles and iron them in place. Use a cool iron and test it on a small scrap of felt beforehand to avoid melting the felt. Machine sew round the outside, close to the edge, to secure the baubles.

6 Make a felt hanging loop using the 3cm (1¼in) wide felt piece, following the instructions on page 16.

7 Place the stocking front and back pieces right sides together and pin. Trap the hanging loop between the layers and sew together with a 1cm (⅜in) seam allowance with backstitch at the beginning and end of the seam.

8 Clip the curves, trim the point of the stocking and turn through. Push the curves and point through gently to form a neat silhouette. At the top of the stocking, fold 1cm (⅜in) over towards the inside of stocking and pin. Sew in place 3mm (⅛in) from the edge to finish.

Snowflake Appliqué

Materials

- ♥ stocking pattern B (without cuff)
- ♥ templates 1 and 2 (page 57)
- ♥ fabric for outer stocking 39 x 66cm (15½ x 26in)
- ♥ felt for hanging loop, 4 x 15cm (1½ x 6in)
- ♥ fabric for lining, 39 x 66cm (15½ x 26in)
- ♥ two colours of felt, 20 x 30cm (8 x 12in)
- ♥ white embroidery thread/floss
- ♥ thread

Tools

- ♥ scissors
- ♥ pins
- ♥ sewing machine
- ♥ embroidery needle

1 Take your stocking outer fabric and fold it in half, right sides together. Pin on stocking pattern B and cut it out, leaving out the cuff part. Repeat with the lining fabric.

2 Take templates 1 and 2 from page 57. Cut out two of template 1 and two of template 2 in each of your felt colours, so you end up with eight circles.

3 Take your stocking front piece and arrange the felt circles, pinning them in place. Machine sew them on, close to the edge of the felt.

4 With white embroidery thread, use running stitch to embroider snowflake motifs inside the felt circles. See the motifs on page 64 for snowflake inspiration.

5 Make a hanging loop with the small piece of felt, as described on page 16.

6 Referring to pages 12–16, place the front of your stocking and the corresponding lining piece right sides together and pin along the top edge. Sew together with a 1cm (³/₈in) seam allowance. Repeat for the back of the stocking. Press the seams towards the toe end of the outer fabric.

7 Pin the front and back pieces together, matching the seams and trapping the hanging loop between the front and back layers. Sew round the stocking, backstitching at the beginning and end of the seam line. Remember to leave a gap in the lining big enough to fit your hand through.

8 Clip the curves, trim the point at the toe of the stocking and turn through. Gently manipulate the stocking so that all curves are smooth and push through the point. Hand sew the opening in the lining closed. Push the lining into the stocking, making sure to push it fully into the toe. Press gently, avoiding the felt.

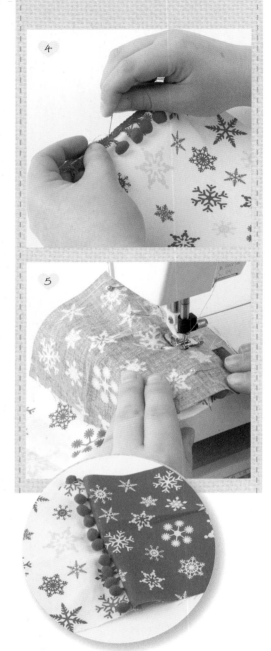

Pompom Cuff

Materials

- stocking pattern A (with straight cuff)
- fabric for outer stocking, 52 x 66cm (20½ x 26in)
- contrast fabric for cuff, 45 x 17cm (17½ x 6¾in)
- fabric for hanging loop, 4 x 15cm (1½ x 6in)
- fabric for lining, 41 x 66cm (16 x 26in)
- two 20cm (8in) lengths of pompom trim
- thread

Tools

- scissors
- pins
- sewing machine
- needle and thread for tacking

1 Take the stocking outer fabric, fold in half, right sides together and pin on stocking pattern A (with cuff). Cut out, using the straight-edged guideline for the cuff.

2 Fold the lining fabric in half, right sides together, pin on stocking pattern A and cut out, this time leaving out the cuff part.

3 Fold the cuff fabric in half, right sides together, and pin on the cuff part of pattern A. Cut out the cuffs.

4 Take the outer fabric stocking and tack/baste pompom trim to the top of both stocking pieces.

5 Take the cuff pieces and pin them to the stocking, right sides together, sandwiching the pompom trim inside. Sew together, backstitching at the beginning and end of the seam line with a 1cm (³⁄₈in) seam allowance. Repeat for the back of the stocking.

6 Take the lining pieces and pin them to the top of the cuff/stocking pieces, right sides together. Sew in place with a 1cm (³⁄₈in) seam allowance.

7 Make a hanging loop with the 4cm (1½in) piece of fabric, as shown on pages 13–14.

8 Place the stocking front/lining piece and the stocking back/lining pieces right sides together and pin in place, sandwiching the hanging loop between the layers (see page 14). Sew round the stocking with a 1cm (³⁄₈in) seam allowance, remembering to leave a gap in the lining big enough to fit your hand through. Backstitch at the beginning and end of the seam line.

9 Clip curves on the outer and lining fabric and turn through. Push through all curves and gently manipulate the stocking into shape. Hand sew the opening in the lining closed. Push the lining into the stocking, making sure to push it fully into the toe. Fold the stocking cuff over, making sure no lining is showing. Gently press, avoiding the pompoms.

Mini Initial

Materials

- stocking pattern C
- templates 6 and 7 (page 59)
- fabric for outer of stocking, 32 x 22cm (12½ x 8¾ in)
- hessian, 12 x 6cm (4¾ x 2⅜in)
- embroidery thread in a contrasting colour
- wooden button
- two 25cm (10in) pieces of twine/cord for drawstring
- thread

Tools

- scissors
- pinking shears (optional)
- embroidery needle
- sewing machine
- pins
- pencil
- iron

1 Take your stocking fabric and fold it in half, right sides together. Pin on stocking pattern C and cut it out. Pin template 7 (the smaller tag shape) onto the remaining fabric and cut out one shape. Pin template 6 (the larger tag shape) onto the hessian and cut it out.

2 Pin the two stocking pieces right sides together and with a pin or pencil, mark 6cm (2⅜in) down from the top of the stocking on both sides. Sew the stocking together with a 1cm (⅜in) seam allowance, starting and finishing at these points, remembering to backstitch at the start and finish of the seam. As this stocking is unlined, to prevent fraying you might like to use pinking shears or a zigzag stitch to neaten the raw edges.

3 To create the channel for the drawstring, press the remainder of the seam allowance (at the sides above the 6cm marked points) over by 5mm (¼in).

4 At the top of the stocking, fold over 1cm (⅜in) towards the wrong side, and press. Then fold down again to just above the seam line, press and pin in place.

5 Repeat for the reverse of the stocking. Sew in place 3mm (⅛in) from the fold. Turn the stocking through and press.

6 For the drawstring, take the lengths of twine and feed one from left to right through the channel and then continue through the back channel from right to left. Knot the ends together. Repeat with the other piece of twine, working from right to left.

7 For the initial tag, take the hessian and fabric tag pieces. Pin the fabric tag centrally on top of the hessian. Machine sew in place 3mm (⅛in) from the fabric edge. With the contrasting embroidery thread, hand sew your choice of initial onto the tag with running stitch. Hand sew the tag to the front of the stocking and finish with the wooden button detail.

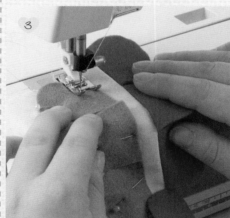

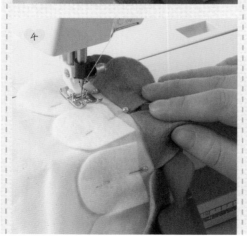

Scalloped Felt

Materials

- ♥ stocking pattern A (without cuff)
- ♥ template 8 (page 58)
- ♥ main fabric, 46 x 66cm (18 x 26in)
- ♥ three colours of felt, each 30 x 30cm (11¾ x 11¾in) with approximately thirty-two scallops cut from each colour using template 8, page 58)
- ♥ piece of felt, 3 x 15cm (1¼ x 6in)
- ♥ piece of felt, 5 x 42cm (2 x 16½in)
- ♥ thread

Tools

- ♥ scissors
- ♥ pinking shears (optional)
- ♥ pins
- ♥ sewing machine

1 Take your main fabric and fold it in half, right sides together. Pin on stocking pattern A and cut it out, leaving out the cuff part. Take one of your stocking pieces and, with your first felt colour, pin a line of scallops across the top of the stocking, lining up the straight edges at the tops of the scallops with the top of the stocking. You may find it easier to centralise one scallop on the stocking and work outwards to the edges.

2 Sew along the top of the scallop pieces 5mm (¼in) from the edge of the felt.

3 Take your next colour of felt scallops and, folding the first line back, pin in place 1cm (³⁄₈in) from the first line. Stagger the scallops so that the edge of one scallop lines up with the middle of a scallop in the previous row. Sew as before.

4 Repeat with the third colour of felt, lining up with the original row of scallops. Continue sewing the three colours until the whole stocking is covered.

5 Make a hanging loop from the 3cm (1¼in) wide felt piece (see page 16).

6 Pin the stocking front and back right sides together. Sandwich the hanging loop on the right-hand side of the stocking, approximately 4cm (1½in) from the top.

7 Sew round the stocking edge, backstitching at the beginning and end of the seam line and using a 1cm (³⁄₈in) seam allowance. This stocking is unlined, so either trim the raw edges with pinking shears or use a machine zigzag stitch to neaten the edges.

8 Turn through to the right side and press lightly with a cool iron. Test on a scrap piece of the felt first, as some felt is completely synthetic and may melt at high temperatures.

9 Take the 5cm (2in) wide piece of felt. Fold the felt in half over the top of the stocking to cover the raw edge, starting at the back, just past either seam. Pin in place. Where the ends meet, overlap the felt and pin in place. Sew the felt trim in place, approximately 5mm (¼in) from the edge, backstitching at the beginning and end of the seam line.

Stitched Tree

Materials

- stocking pattern A (without cuff)
- fabric for outer stocking, 41 x 66cm (16 x 26in)
- fabric for hanging loop, 4 x 15cm (1½ x 6in)
- fabric for lining, 41 x 66cm (16 x 26in)
- embroidery thread in green, brown and yellow
- small buttons
- thread

Tools

- scissors
- sewing machine
- pins
- embroidery needle
- pencil
- iron

1 Take your stocking outer fabric and fold it in half, right sides together. Pin on stocking pattern A and cut out, leaving out the cuff part. Repeat with the lining fabric.

2 On the right side of one of the stocking outer pieces, embroider a vertical row of running stitch with brown embroidery thread. This will form the trunk of your tree. You may wish to mark the line with a light pencil or pins to guide you.

3 Next, using a shade of green, embroider the branches, starting with narrow branches at the top of the tree and gradually increasing in width as you near the bottom. Secure all loose ends at the back.

4 For the decorations, use a selection of small buttons, attached with embroidery thread. I have used a mixture of mother-of-pearl, wooden and neutral shirt buttons for a rustic look. With yellow thread, embroider a simple eight-point star on top of the tree.

5 Make a hanging loop with the 4cm (1½in) strip of fabric as shown on pages 13–14.

6 Place the front of your stocking and the corresponding lining piece right sides together and pin along the top edge. Sew together with a 1cm (³⁄₈in) seam allowance. Repeat for the back of the stocking.

7 Press the seam allowances towards the toe end of the outer fabric.

8 Pin the front and back pieces together, matching seams and trapping the hanging loop between the front and back layers (see page 14). Sew round the stocking, backstitching at the beginning and end of the seam line. Leave a gap in the lining big enough for your hand.

9 Clip the curves and turn through. Gently manipulate the stocking so that all curves are smooth. Hand sew the opening in the lining closed. Push the lining into the stocking, making sure to push it fully into the toe. Press gently.

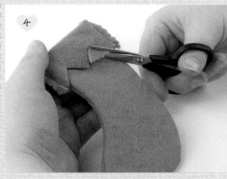

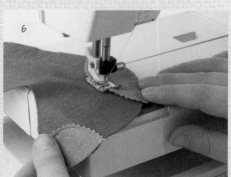

Advent Calendar

Materials

- stocking pattern C
- templates 9 and 10 (page 58)
- twelve pieces of felt in two colours, 22 x 32cm (9 x 12½in)
- twelve pieces of fabric in two colours/ designs, 22 x 32cm (9 x 12½in)
- a selection of trimmings of your choice: ric-rac, felt offcuts, ribbon etc
- fusible web
- pegs
- thread

Tools

- scissors
- pinking shears (optional)
- sewing machine
- pins
- iron

This project creates a variety of simple mini stockings, some plain, some simply embellished. There is guidance below, but you could further personalise yours with letters, numbers or motifs of your choice.

1 Take one of the felt pieces and fold it in half, right sides together. Using stocking pattern C, cut out six pairs of the mini stocking. Repeat with the remaining felt piece and the two fabric pieces, so you have twenty-four stocking pairs in total.

2 Cut a variety of motifs from the leftover felt and fabric, using templates 9 and 10 on page 58 or your own imagination.

3 To construct the plain fabric stockings: pin two stocking pieces right sides together and sew around with a 1cm (³⁄₈in) seam allowance. Trim the seam allowance with pinking shears if you have them. Turn over 2cm (¾in) at the top and sew round the top of the stocking 1cm (³⁄₈in) from the edge. Turn the stocking through.

4 To construct the felt stockings: pin two stocking pieces right sides together and sew around with a 1cm (³⁄₈in) seam allowance. Trim the seam allowance with pinking shears if you have them. Turn over 2cm (¾in) at the top and sew round the top of the stocking, 1cm (³⁄₈in) from the edge. Alternatively, create a fold-over cuff by turning the stocking through and folding 2cm (¾in) over to the right side. Trim into a zigzag shape with scissors if desired.

5 For the fabric appliqué: iron fusible web onto the reverse of the appliqué fabric, draw round the motif template or cut out an image from the design of the fabric, remove the backing and iron on to the background fabric/felt. Sew round the motif.

6 There is no need to use fusible web for the felt appliqué, as felt is a quite a stable fabric. Simply pin and stitch the felt pieces in place. Draw round the motif templates or trace the toe/heel templates from stocking pattern C. You can also sew strips of felt or fabric, layered with ric-rac or ribbon across the stocking, about 6cm (2³⁄₈in) from the top.

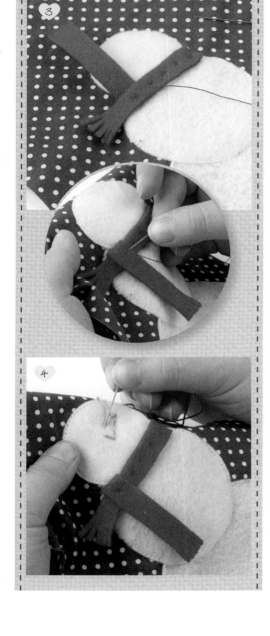

Snowman

Materials

- stocking pattern A (without cuff)
- templates 2, 3, 11 and 12 (pages 57–59)
- fabric for outer stocking, 41 x 66cm (16 x 26in) and for hanging loop, 4 x 15cm (1½ x 6in)
- fabric for lining, 41 x 66cm (16 x 26in)
- white felt, 30 x 30cm (11¾ x 11¾in)
- black felt 8 x 8cm (3 x 3 in)
- two pieces of red felt, 1 x 7cm (³⁄₈ x 2¾in)
- black and red thread
- orange and silver embroidery thread

Tools

- scissors
- pins
- sewing machine
- embroidery needle
- iron

1 Fold the outer stocking fabric in half, right sides together. Pin on stocking pattern A and cut it out, leaving out the cuff part. Repeat with the lining fabric.

2 Cut one or two pieces of white felt freehand to form a snow-covered hill. Pin in place on the stocking front and machine stitch around the outside, close to the edge. Use templates 2, 3 and 11 to cut three circles from the white felt to form the snowman. Arrange on the 'hill', pin and sew in place close to the circles' edges.

3 Take the red felt pieces to form the scarf. Snip into one end of each piece to create fringing. Place one piece vertically at the edge of the snowman's neck and sew in place with a couple of small stitches. Place the other piece horizontally and sew in place with tiny stitches, leaving the ends free to create movement. Make sure you cover the end of the first piece. Fold the first piece over the top of the horizontal piece and sew in place.

4 Using orange embroidery thread, hand sew a carrot nose with running stitch. Sew the outline and fill it in with smaller stitches.

5 Using template 12, cut the snowman's hat from black felt and pin and hand sew it in place with black thread. Next, snip tiny pieces of black felt and hand sew with small stitches to make coal eyes, mouth and buttons for the snowman.

6 With the silver thread, hand sew some simple snowflakes for extra detail.

7 Make a hanging loop as shown on pages 13–14. Pin the front of your stocking and the corresponding lining piece right sides together along the top edge. Sew together with a 1cm (³⁄₈in) seam allowance. Repeat for the back of the stocking. Press the seams towards the toe end of the outer fabric.

8 Pin the front and back pieces together, matching seams and trapping the hanging loop between front and back layers. Sew round the stocking in the usual way, remembering to leave a gap in the lining big enough to fit your hand through.

9 Clip curves and turn the stocking out. Gently manipulate the stocking so that all curves are smooth. Hand sew the opening in the lining closed. Push the lining into the stocking, making sure to push it fully into the toe. Press gently.

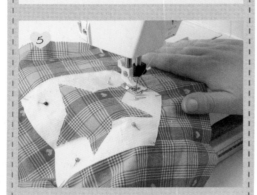

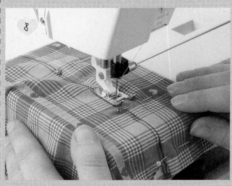

Toy Sack

Materials

- stocking pattern D
- templates 13 and 14 (page 60)
- fabric for stocking, 75 x 95cm (29½ x 37in)
- contrast fabric, 30 x 30cm (11¾ x 11¾in) for pocket, heel and toe
- fusible web, 12 x 12cm (4¾ x 4¾in)
- two 1m (1 yard) pieces of twine, ribbon or cord
- thread

Tools

- scissors and pinking shears
- pins
- sewing machine

1 Fold the stocking fabric in half, right sides together. Pin on stocking pattern D and cut out.

2 Trace the heel and toe from your stocking pattern piece. Pin the pocket pattern piece (template 13), heel and toe on your contrast fabric and cut out.

3 Take the pocket piece and with pinking shears, trim what will become the top edge of the pocket. Fold over 2cm (¾in) to the wrong side and press in place. Sew a line of stitching across the top of the pocket about 1.5cm (½in) from the top. Press all other sides over by 1cm (⅜in) to the wrong side.

4 Apply the fusible web to a leftover piece of the outer fabric. Draw round the star motif (template 14) and cut out. Remove the backing from the star and iron in place. Sew around the edge of the motif.

5 Pin the pocket in place and sew all round it, close to the edge, leaving the top open. Backstitch at the beginning and end of the seam line. Repeat 1cm (⅜in) from first stitching line.

6 Pin and sew the toe and heel to the stocking front, about 3mm (⅛in) from the edge.

7 Pin the stocking pieces right sides together. Mark 12cm (4¾in) down from the top of the fabric on each side. Sew the stocking together, beginning and ending at these points, and backstitching at the beginning and end. As this stocking is unlined, to prevent fraying you can use pinking shears or a zigzag stitch to neaten the raw edges.

8 To create the channel for the drawstring, press the remainder of the seam allowance (above the marked points) over by 1cm (⅜in). At the top of the stocking, fold over 1cm (⅜in) towards the wrong side, and press. Then fold down again to just above the seam line, press and pin in place. Repeat for the reverse of the stocking. Sew in place 3mm (⅛in) from the fold. Turn the stocking through and press.

9 Take one length of drawstring and thread through the front channel from left to right, then continue threading through the back channel from right to left so both ends are on the left hand side. Knot together. Repeat with the second length, from right to left.

Tip

To create a rustic drawstring to match the fabric, I plaited lengths of multicoloured twine, knotting at each end. You could use cord or ribbon for a simpler look.

Upcycled Sweater

Materials

- ♥ old sweater/cardigan (Fair Isle is good)
- ♥ stocking pattern B (without cuff)
- ♥ thread

Tools

- ♥ scissors
- ♥ sewing machine
- ♥ pins

1 Lay the sweater flat and place stocking pattern B (cut out without the cuff) on top. Place the top of the stocking pattern at the edge of the sweater, to make use of the finished edge of the sweater. If the sweater has buttons, line up the centre of the pattern with the buttons. Pin in place.

2 Cut out, through both the back and front of the sweater, to make both sides of the stocking.

3 To make a hanging loop, cut a 4 x 15cm (1½ x 6in) piece from the leftover sweater, fold it in half lengthwise, wrong sides together, and sew together about 5mm (¼in) from the raw edges.

4 Place the stocking pieces right sides together, sandwiching the hanging loop between the layers, and machine sew round the edge with a short stitch length, backstitching at the beginning and end of the seam line.

5 Turn through and manipulate the seam to create a rounded shape. Push the toe through gently.

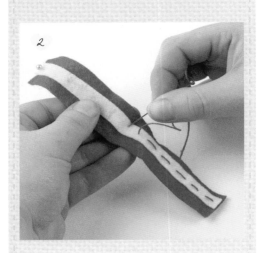

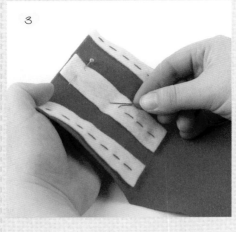

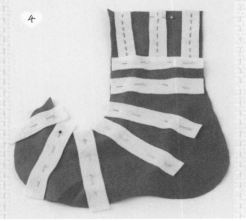

Hand-Stitched Felt

Materials

- stocking pattern B (without cuff)
- felt for stocking 39 x 66cm (15⅜ x 26in)
- white felt, 30 x 20cm (11¾ x 8in)
- red embroidery thread

Tools

- scissors
- embroidery needle
- pins

1 Take the felt for the stocking, fold it in half, pin stocking pattern B in place and cut out, leaving out the cuff part. From the leftover felt, cut a piece 15 x 3cm (6 x 1¼in) for the hanging loop. From the white felt, cut a strip 1 x 15cm (⅜ x 6in).

2 To create the hanging loop, arrange the white felt strip along the middle of the piece of red felt and secure with running stitch in red embroidery thread. Set aside.

3 Cut three pieces of white felt 10 x 2.5cm (4 x 1in) and pin them to the front of the stocking vertically – centre one piece and arrange the others on each side. Secure with running stitch down the centre of each strip using the red embroidery thread.

4 Cut seven pieces of white felt 2.5cm x 13cm (1 x 5⅛in). Lay one across the bottom of the vertical stripes, overlapping slightly, and pin in place. Arrange and pin the remaining pieces around the stocking.

5 Sew all the pieces in place with running stitch in the red embroidery thread.

6 Trace the heel pattern from pattern piece B, place it on the remaining white felt and cut out the shape. Use the red embroidery thread to sew it in place on the stocking front with running stitch.

7 Trim all excess white felt away to create a clean stocking shape, making sure not to cut through any stitches.

8 Take the stocking front and back and pin wrong sides together, sandwiching the hanging loop between them. Sew the layers together with running stitch in red embroidery thread about 3mm (⅛in) from the edge.

Quilted Patchwork

Materials

- stocking pattern B (without cuff)
- selection of fabric pieces, 12.5 x 6.5cm (5 x 2½in)
- fabric for reverse, 39 x 33cm (15⅜ x 13in)
- wadding/batting, 39 x 33cm (15⅜ x 13in)
- lining fabric, 39 x 66cm (15⅜ x 26in)
- thread

Tools

- scissors
- pins
- sewing machine
- iron

1 Take two of the fabric pieces and pin them right sides together along the short side. Sew them together with a 1cm (⅜in) seam allowance. Repeat until you have joined four pieces together in a long line. Press the seams to one side.

2 Repeat with another set of pieces. Take the two strips and pin then sew them right sides together along the long side, placing the join of two pieces against the centre of another to create a staggered, brickwork effect. Press the horizontal seams downwards.

3 Continue sewing staggered strips until you have a piece of fabric large enough for stocking pattern B. Place the stocking pattern on the patchwork and cut it out, leaving out the cuff part. Cut the back of the stocking, flipping over the pattern first.

4 Take the wadding/batting, pin the patchwork panel in place, right side up, on top. To quilt the panel, sew in straight lines along the horizontal joins of the fabric.

5 To make the hanging loop, take one of the leftover fabric rectangles and sew together as described on pages 13–14.

6 Use the same stocking pattern to cut out two lining pieces, leaving out the cuff part. Pin the stocking front and the corresponding lining piece right sides together, along the top edge. Sew together with a 1cm (⅜in) seam allowance. Repeat for the back of the stocking. Press the seams towards the toe of the outer fabric.

7 Pin the front and back pieces together, matching the seams and trapping the hanging loop between the front and back. Sew round the stocking, backstitching at the beginning and end of the seam line. Remember to leave a gap in the lining big enough to fit your hand through.

8 Clip the curves and turn through. Gently manipulate the stocking so that all the curves are smooth. Hand sew the opening in the lining closed. Push the lining into the stocking, making sure to push it fully into the toe. Press gently.

Ric-Rac Panels

Materials

- ♥ stocking pattern A (without cuff)
- ♥ main fabric 35 x 30cm (13¾ x 11¾in)
- ♥ contrasting fabric 35 x 30cm (13¾ x 11¾in)
- ♥ fabric for reverse, 41 x 33cm (16⅛ x 13in)
- ♥ lining fabric, 41cm x 66cm
- ♥ fabric for hanging loop, 4 x 16cm (1½ x 6¼in)
- ♥ 1.8m (5ft 11in) of ric-rac
- ♥ thread

Tools

- ♥ scissors
- ♥ pins
- ♥ sewing machine

1 Cut five strips of each of the two fabrics measuring 32 x 6cm (12⅝ x 2⅜in). Place stocking pattern A right side down on the reverse fabric, pin and cut out, leaving out the cuff part. Fold the lining fabric in half, right sides together, pin on the stocking pattern and cut out.

2 Take one main and one contrasting strip and pin then stitch them right sides together along the long side with a 1cm (³⁄₈in) seam allowance. Press the seam allowances down towards the bottom of the pattern. Repeat this step, sewing alternate strips together until you have a piece of fabric big enough for stocking pattern A. Pin the pattern on right side up and cut it out, leaving out the cuff part.

3 Cut lengths of ric-rac and pin and sew them in place across each seam line, until all the seams are covered.

4 Make the hanging loop as described on pages 13–14.

5 Pin the front and back pieces right sides together, matching the seams and sandwiching the hanging loop between the front and back layers. Sew round the stocking, remembering to leave a gap in the lining big enough to fit your hand through, and backstitch at the beginning and end of the seam line.

6 Clip the curves and turn the stocking the right way out. Gently manipulate the stocking so that all the curves are smooth. Hand-sew the opening in the lining closed. Push the lining into the stocking, making sure to push it fully into the toe. Press gently.

Hessian Initial

Materials

- stocking pattern A (with cuff)
- hessian, 52 x 66cm (20½ x 26in)
- contrast fabric, 30cm (11¾in) square
- lining fabric, 41 x 66cm (16 x 26in)
- fusible web, 10cm (4in) square
- felt for pocket, 10cm (4in) square
- felt for hanging loop, 3 x 15cm (1¼ x 6in)
- thread

Tools

- scissors
- pins
- sewing machine

1 Fold the hessian in half, pin on stocking pattern A and cut out, including the cuff. Fold the contrast fabric in half, right sides together, and pin on the cuff part of stocking pattern A. Cut out, saving the spare fabric. Fold the lining fabric in half, right sides together and pin on stocking pattern A. Cut it out, leaving out the cuff part this time.

2 Iron fusible web onto the back of the spare contrast fabric piece, sketch out your chosen initial (in reverse) and cut out. Remove the backing and iron the initial lightly onto the felt pocket piece. Carefully sew around the letter to secure it.

3 Position the pocket in the centre of the stocking front and sew it in place around three sides, leaving the top open.

4 Trace the heel and toe from stocking pattern A. Pin them on your remaining contrast fabric and cut them out. Pin and sew them to the stocking front, close to the edge.

5 Make the hanging loop from the felt piece (see page 16).

6 Take the contrast cuff and pin it to the top of the stocking outer front. Sew it in place and press the seam towards the toe. Repeat for the reverse of the stocking.

7 Place the front of your stocking and the corresponding lining piece right sides together and pin along the top edge. Sew together. Repeat for the back of the stocking. Press the seams towards the toe of the outer fabric.

8 Pin the front and back pieces together, matching seams and trapping the hanging loop between the front and lining layers. Sew around the stocking, remembering to leave a gap in the lining big enough to fit your hand through. Backstitch at the beginning and end of the seam line.

9 Clip the curves and turn the stocking right way out. Push all the curves into shape. Hand sew the opening in the lining closed. Push the lining into the stocking, making sure to push it fully into the toe. Fold the cuff over, making sure no lining is visible. Press.

Appliqué Trees

Materials

- stocking pattern A (without cuff)
- outer fabric, 41 x 66cm (16⅛ x 26in)
- lining fabric, 41 x 66cm (16⅛ x 26in)
- templates 15, 16, 17 and 18 (pages 60–62)
- fabrics for trees
- fusible web
- felt for hanging loop, 3 x 15cm (1¼ x 6in)
- ric-rac, ribbon and embroidery threads
- fabric for grass, 35 x 20cm (13¾ x 8in)
- thread

Tools

- scissors
- pins
- sewing machine
- iron

1 Take the outer fabric and fold it in half, right sides together, then pin on and cut out stocking pattern A, leaving out the cuff part. Repeat for the lining fabric. Take the fusible web and iron it onto the reverse of your chosen tree fabrics. Use the templates to cut out five or six trees.

2 Cut a freehand curve from the grass fabric and sew it in place at the bottom of the stocking front.

3 Machine stitch wavy lines over the grass, catching green and gold embroidery threads as you sew.

4 Take your fabric trees, remove the backing paper and arrange on the stocking front. Iron them in place and machine stitch round the edges to secure them. At this point you can also add ric-rac, ribbon or embroidery thread details for extra interest.

5 To make the hanging loop, fold the felt in half lengthwise, place a length of ric-rac over the top and sew it all together, close to the edge.

6 Place the front of the stocking and the corresponding lining piece right sides together and pin then sew along the top edge. Repeat for the back of the stocking. Press the seams down towards the toe of the outer fabric.

7 Pin the front and back pieces together, matching seams and trapping the hanging loop between the front and lining layers. Sew round the stocking, remembering to leave a gap in the lining big enough to fit your hand through. Backstitch at the beginning and end of the seam line.

8 Clip the curves and turn the stocking the right way out. Push all the curves into shape. Hand sew the opening in the lining closed. Push the lining into the stocking, making sure to push it fully into the toe. Press.

Gorgeous Gifts

Materials

- stocking pattern A (with pointed cuff)
- outer fabric, 52 x 66cm (20½ x 26in)
- lining fabric, 52 x 66cm (20½ x 26in)
- template 19 (page 63)
- four contrasting fabrics for gifts and cuff, each 25cm (10in) square
- ribbons and ric-rac
- fusible web
- thread

Tools

- scissors
- pins
- sewing machine

1 Fold the outer fabric in half, right sides together. Pin on stocking pattern A and cut it out, including the pointed cuff. Fold the lining fabric in half, right sides together, pin on stocking pattern A again and cut out, this time without a cuff.

2 Iron fusible web onto the back of the contrasting fabrics and draw gift shapes freehand. Make sure you leave enough fabric for the pointed cuff. Remove the backing paper and arrange the gifts on the stocking front. Iron to secure and stitch in place, close to the edge. You can top stitch lengths of ribbon and ric-rac to add details to the gifts. Leave loose ends of ribbon to tie into bows if you wish.

3 To construct the pointed cuff, take your contrasting fabrics and template 19. Cut out a selection of pieces. You will need four pieces for the front: two with the point on the left, two with it on the right, and the same again for the back of the stocking.

4 Sew four pieces together with a 1cm (⅜in) seam allowance, making sure you have a point on the left and right (see picture). Press the seams open. Repeat with the remaining pieces.

5 Take the outer front piece and pin the pointed cuff patchwork piece to the pointed cuff, right sides together. Sew together them along the zig-zag side only with a 1cm (⅜in) seam allowance. Trim the seam allowance down to 5mm (¼in) and clip the points. Turn through and press. Repeat for the back. Attach the lining along the top edge.

6 Cut a 4 x 15cm (1½ x 6in) piece from the leftover contrasting fabrics and make a hanging loop as shown on pages 13–14.

7 Place the stocking pieces right sides together and pin, trapping the hanging loop between the layers on the outer cuff. Sew together carefully and don't forget to leave a gap for turning through in the lining.

8 Clip the curves and turn through. Push all the curves into shape. Hand sew the opening in the lining closed. Push the lining into the stocking, making sure to push it fully into the toe. Fold over the cuff. Press.

Pompoms
Galore

Materials

- pattern piece B (with cuff)
- outer fabric, 49 x 66cm (19¼ x 26in)
- lining fabric, 39 x 66cm (15⅜ x 26in)
- 1m (1 yard) of pompom trim
- thread

Tools

- scissors
- needle and thread for tacking
- pins
- sewing machine
- iron

1 Fold the outer fabric in half, right sides together, pin on stocking pattern B and cut out, including the cuff. Also cut out another piece, just from the cuff part. Cut a piece 4 x 15cm (1½ x 6in) from the leftover fabric for the hanging loop. Fold the lining fabric in half, right sides together, pin on pattern piece B and cut out, this time leaving out the cuff part.

2 Take the stocking and cuff pieces and pin them right sides together, making sure the cuff fabric will be the right way up when the cuff is folded over (see picture). Sew them with a 1cm (⅜in) seam allowance and press the seam down towards the toe.

3 Pin the other side of the cuff to the lining, right sides together, and sew with a 1cm (⅜in) seam allowance. Press.

4 Make the hanging loop as shown on pages 13–14.

5 Take the stocking front piece and mark 11cm (4¼in) down from the cuff seam on both sides. Starting and finishing at this point, tack/baste the pompom trim to the edge with the pompoms pointing inwards.

6 Pin the stocking pieces right sides together, trapping the hanging loop between the layers on the outer cuff. Sew together carefully with a 1cm (⅜in) seam allowance, avoiding the pompoms. Don't forget to leave a gap in the lining for turning through.

7 Clip the curves, trim the points and turn through (see page 15). Push all the curves into shape. Hand sew the opening in the lining closed. Push the lining into the stocking, making sure to push it fully into the toe. Fold over the cuff. Press gently, avoiding the pompoms.

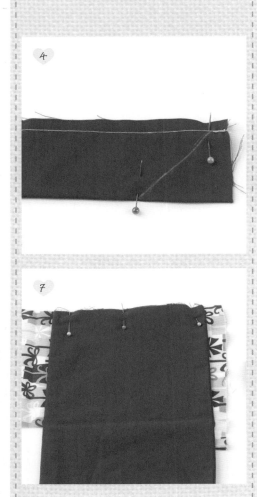

Big Bow

Materials

- stocking pattern A (without cuff)
- outer fabric, 41 x 66cm (16 x 26in)
- fabric for hanging loop, 4 x 15cm (1½ x 6in)
- lining fabric, 41 x 66cm (16 x 26in)
- two pieces of coordinating plain fabric, 18 x 24cm (7 x 9½in) for the bow
- one piece of coordinating plain fabric, 12 x 7cm (4¾ x 2¾in)
- one piece of coordinating plain fabric, 50 x 12cm (19¾ x 4¾)
- thread

Tools

- pins
- scissors
- sewing machine
- needle and thread (optional)
- iron

1 Fold the stocking outer fabric in half, right sides together. Pin on stocking pattern A and cut out, leaving out the cuff part. Repeat with the lining fabric.

2 Pin the 18cm (7in) long pieces right sides together and sew down each long side with a 1cm (³⁄₈in) seam allowance to create a tube, backstitching at both ends. Turn through and press flat.

3 Take the 12 x 7cm (4¾ x 2¾in) piece, fold it in half lengthwise, right sides together and pin in place. Sew down the length with a 1cm (³⁄₈in) seam allowance. Turn through and press. Sew the two short ends together to create a loop for your bow.

4 Fold the 50cm (19¾in) long piece in half lengthwise, right sides together, pin and sew down the length with a 1cm (³⁄₈in) seam allowance to form a long tube. Mark 5cm (2in) from one end at the fold. On the seam side, mark 1cm (³⁄₈in) from the end of the fabric. Draw a line diagonally between the two points and sew along this line to form the point of the bow tails.

5 Trim away excess fabric leaving a 1cm (³⁄₈in) seam allowance. Draw the same line on the opposite end, but do not sew. Trim away the excess as before and·turn the tube through. Carefully push the point through at the closed end. At the open end, press under the 1cm (³⁄₈in) seam allowance to match the other end. Hand sew the opening closed. Press the whole strip.

6 Make the hanging loop with the 4cm (1½in) piece as shown on pages 13–14.

7 Take the stocking front piece and the 18 x 24cm (7 x 9½in) tube. Pin one open side of the tube along the side of the stocking, 2cm (¾in) from the top.

8 Slide the loop over the other open end, then pin this end to the other side of the stocking, again 2cm (¾in) from the top. Tack or sew in place on both sides, 5mm (¼in) from the edge.

9 Pin the front of your stocking and the corresponding lining piece, right sides together, along the top edge. Sew together with a 1cm (³⁄₈in) seam allowance. Repeat for the back of the stocking. Press the seam allowances down towards the toe of the outer fabric.

10 Pin the front and back pieces together, matching seams and trapping the hanging loop between the front and back layers. Sew round the stocking in the usual way, leaving a gap to turn through (see page 15).

11 Clip the curves and turn the stocking through. Manipulate to smooth all the curves. Hand sew the opening in the lining closed. Push the lining into stocking, making sure to push it fully into the toe. Press gently.

12 Take the 'tails' of the bow and push them through the loop, making sure the loop seam is hidden at the back. You can sew a couple of small stitches through all three parts of the bow to keep them in place if you wish.

Templates

The templates are all shown full size. Note that the stocking patterns are on the pattern sheet at the back of the book.

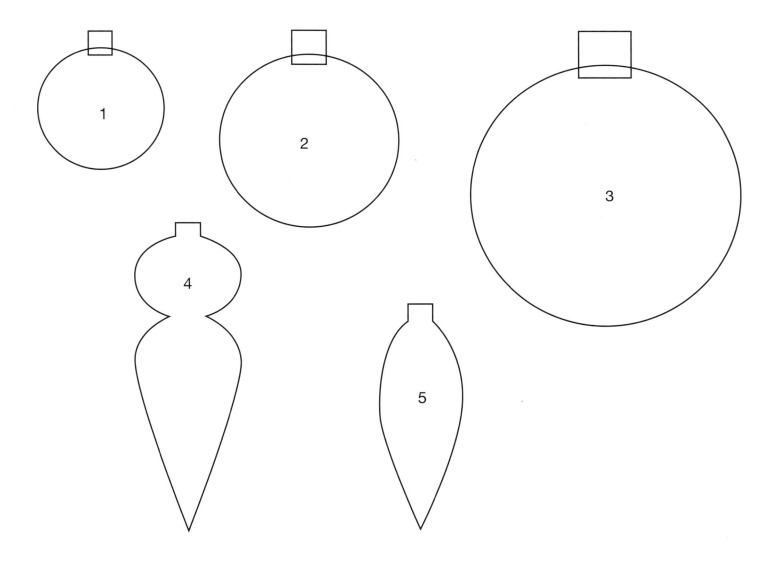

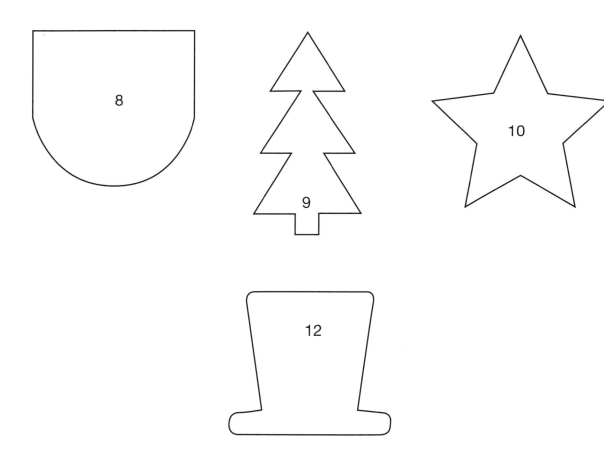

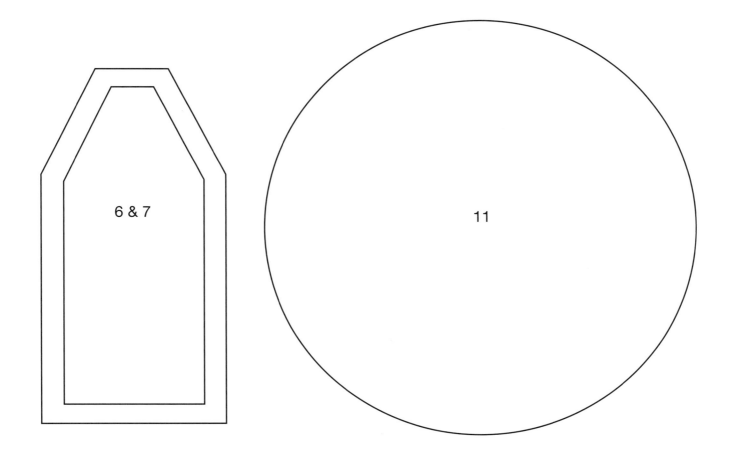

6 & 7

11

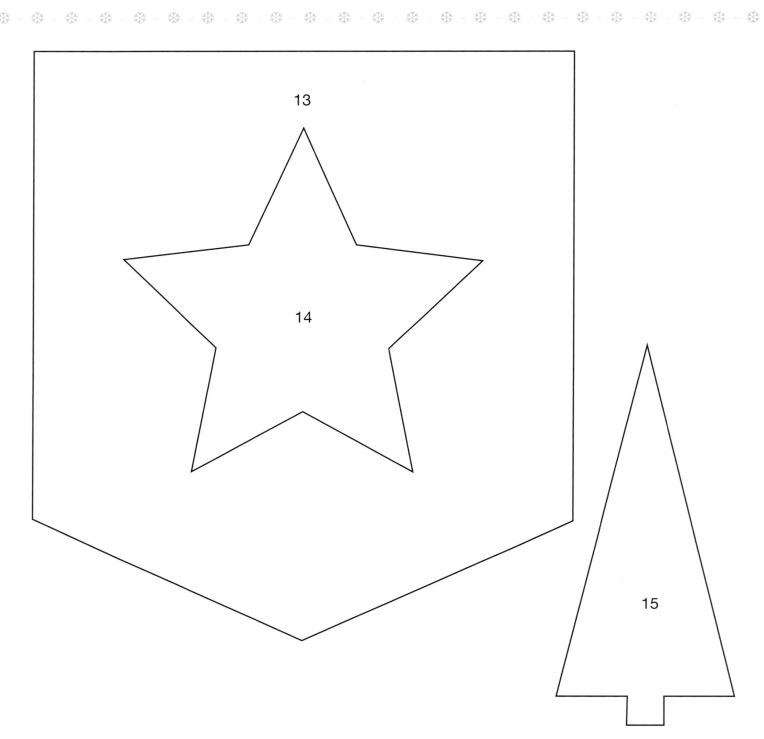

13

14

15

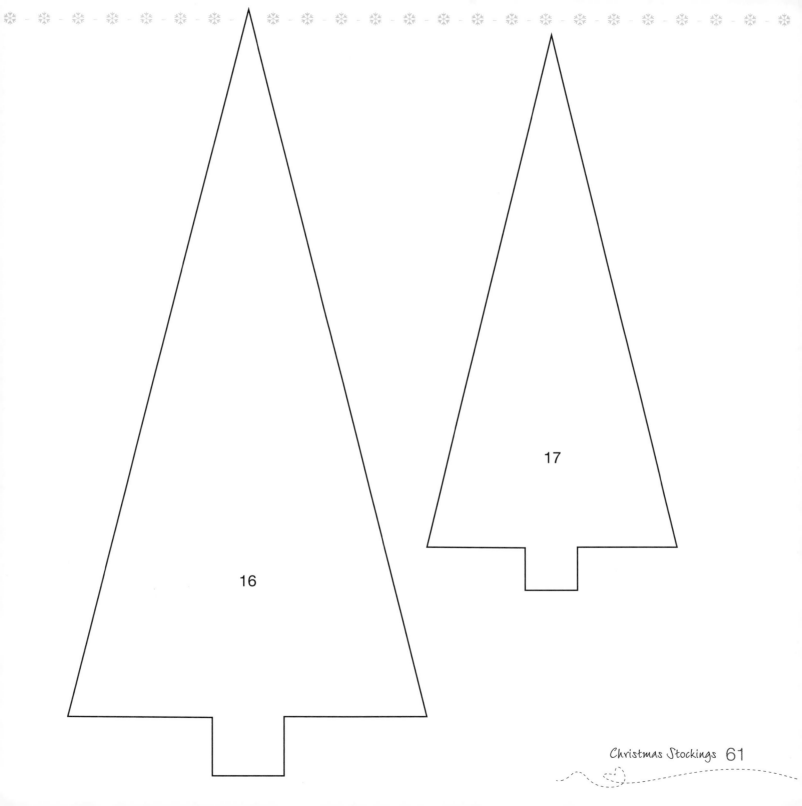

16

17

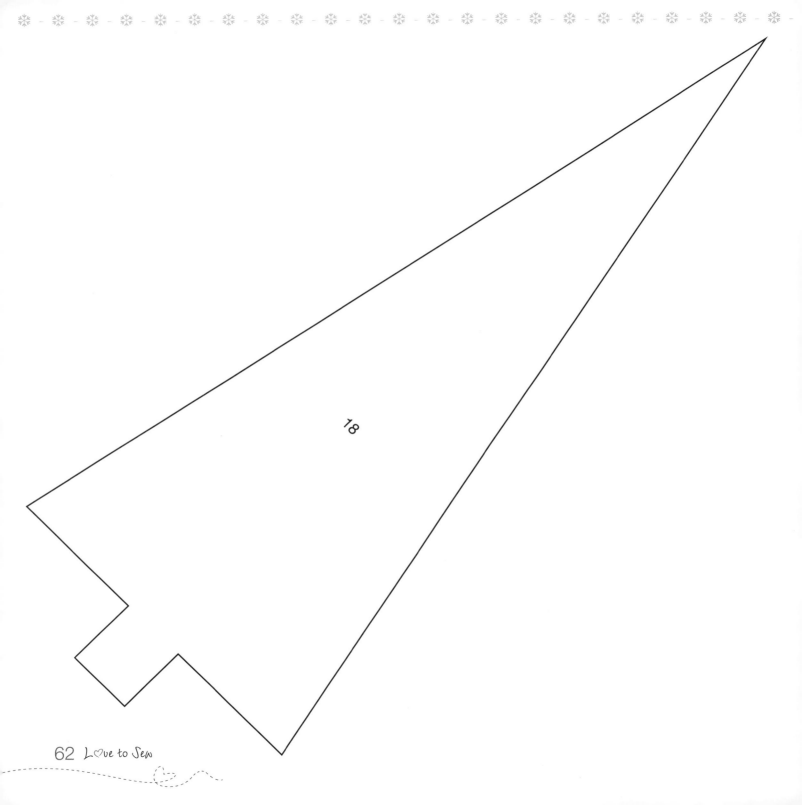

18

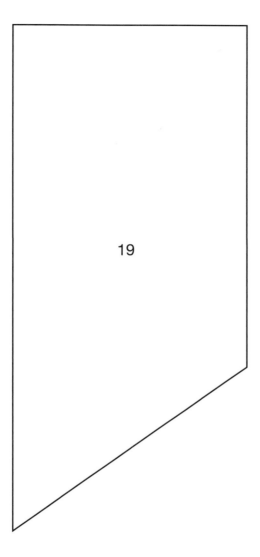

19

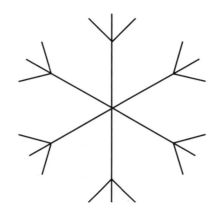

Snowflake motifs

Dedication

This book is dedicated to my wonderful family,
who encourage, support and celebrate all my endeavours.